Fragrance of love

Mariana Zozim

BlueRose ONE
Stories Matter

First Published in May 2022

ISBN: 978-93-93899-22-4

Price: INR 122

BLUEROSE PUBLISHERS

www.bluerosepublishers.com

info@bluerosepublishers.com

+91 8882 898 898

Cover Design:

Geetika

Typographic Design:

Namrata Saini

Illustration Design:

Shreya Kapoor

Distributed by: BlueRose, Amazon, Flipkart

Acknowledgment

I would like to thank God Almighty for giving me an opportunity and a talent to express my feelings and thoughts beautifully. Very special gratitude to my dear friend Subaa Vaishnavi who constantly pushed me to publish my book, her continuous appreciation for my work gave me the courage to step up and do it. I thank my wonderful parents who have always been my backbone and supported me in all of my endeavors. I saved my last gratitude for the best, unique, and marvelous person in my life my elder sister Angela Zozim who is my confidant, whom I can always count on, who always has faith in me and in whatever I do in my life. I will eternally be grateful to all of them.

Dedicated

Fragrance of love is for all my dear readers, I wholeheartedly, Thank you for taking your precious time to read my book. I hope that you enjoy it and will be able to connect to it.

With love,

Mariana Zozim

Preface

"My Mind Knows I Will Never Be Able To Survive,

But My Heart Begins To Beat Stronger When I Found Myself Alive Within Me "

FRAGRANCE OF LOVE

The greatest challenge to us in life starts; when it comes to our feelings for a person that is to deny it or accept it? to love again even when that so-called "love" makes you feel scared and even not to trust the feeling again, these feelings begin to grow adamantly because you challenged yourself to abandon the memories that once gave you a smile upon your face. A happiness that you never felt before and those precious things are now turned into a tragedy.

Some of us pretend, that very form of love never existed in our life because we are afraid to open that side of our wounded heart that can cause unimaginable pain; it starts to ache when we think about that love and its memories. It is always good to remember our love, how much we cared for a person but not to dwell in grief or hatred but to know how much we can love someone It is definite, where there is this purest form of love the feelings never fade it remains as a fragrance in our life.

The fragrance of love - takes you on a journey inside yourself and shows your wounded side of love as a most powerful and sacred form of your love. The transformation of your love to unconditional love, makes you feel like a soldier who protects your love, by holding the memories without any taint, all of this makes us embrace our scars and hold them as our strength, because our love for a person is something to be embraced, not to detest, regret or to be forgotten, it shows how enormous power it holds that it could fight all the hate, bitterness, and the pain if your love is true. The warm reminiscence of your love will make you rise like the sun so bright that it gives light to the entire world, that's how your love is, though it fights many battles inside you it will never fail to arise again.

"*Fragrance of love*" is the fragrance of our feelings. It makes you remember the story of your love that you lost out of chaos, misunderstanding, lack of maturity, and in many other ways. It brings out the voice of your heartbreak, pain, and the other side of your heart that can never dismiss the love you shared with your loved one. The wonderful, untainted memories that you will want to embrace.

Embracing your love and its memories brings the truest form of your love. Your heart beats even stronger because you feel more alive when you honor your love.

"Love travels in the form of both sorrow and happiness and it is not just a two-way street, it is beyond that. "

Contents

Chapter I

Petals of you

We hold the person we love to an incredibly highest position in our heart, and our heart becomes loyal to them even before we realize it and that is why no matter how hard the circumstances or what difficulties we face, we fight to be with that person we love, we never could give up on them. This love could sometimes turn into a bittersweet tale. Petals of you are an expression of happiness, grief, fear, confusion, excitement, affection, desperation, desire, you experience when you are in love.

"My sweetest tale, my tremendous flame,

You burn my voluminous pain,

I'm irrevocably trapped in your

Mesmerizing game ".

Petals Of You

"It's your right to know,

that my mind overflows, with your voice

in my soul that keeps echoing without letting go ".

- Petals of you

"We are miles apart,

but I still think about you at this hour,

that defines where you exist in my heart ".

- Petals of you

"The second you said this is going to end,

there's nothing more I could pretend,

I lost you again, that I can't withstand ".

- Petals of you

“I remember your voice that dwells in my mind,

I feel the touch of your existence in me,

through the whisper of your words behind my ears “.

-Petals of you

"You thawed my heart with your words,

engraved it with your smile,

and kept me waiting for a while ".

- Petals of you

"Renewed with hope,

rewarded by your glances,

that kept me going, without missing my chances ".

Petals of you

"It was Christmas eve,

with a blooming glory of belief,

I saw you standing in the crowd,

I pushed past the crowd to get to you,

it was like a light that twinkles every time I get closer to it.

- Petals of you

"Every step I take,

every move that I make,

it is like a dream from which I am about to wake ".

- Petals of you

"You have become closer to my heart more and more,

you have become closer to my life like none before ".

- Petals of you

"My eyes are moist,

my hands are free without any belief,

that you are parting from me.

I was about to give you my breath, my strength,

my heart, and myself to you,

to live a life with you,

but ended up becoming your lost dream ".

- Petals of you

"My dream, my harmony, you taught me to live without misery,

your arms held me tight,

I wish at that moment my heartbeat stopped to say,

that I will hold you like you did even after I pass away ".

- Petals of you

"You became my morning glory,

like the sun you raised inside me,

without a doubt that kind heart of yours lifted mine,

your love awakens the innocence within me".

- Petals of you

"The forest of my dreams, you trapped me inside your gleam ".

- Petals of you

"In this drizzling rain,

I caught you in my mind with vain.

Amid of your love you kept me inside,

wrapped me with your warm words,

and your breathtaking smile".

- Petals of you

"Your sweet velvet voice keeps haunting my mind,

not willing to resign from the depths of your love,

is my sanity fading?

is my heart racing?

your voice is like a drug it dwells and wipes away the wounds

in my heart,

I'm content with your love ".

-Petals of you

"You were my haven,

my realm of hope,

and was the life of my whole ".

- Petals of you

"You are like an angel in my life,

who always watches out for me,

and I'm entangled in your undying love for me ".

- Petals of you

In your presence,

I stumble,

crumble,

to end up in your arms".

-Petals of you

"My sweetest tale,

my tremendous flame,

you burn my voluminous pain,

I'm irrevocably, trapped in your mesmerizing game ".

- Petals of you

"You are my sweet dangerous lie,

so hard to deny,

in the world of mine ".

- Petals of you

Chapter II

Petals of us

T*he innocence of one's "love"* and *"their pure heart"* witnesses joy in the eyes of their beloved. There are no restrictions, no boundaries for the spirit of true love it is welcomed without any tainted thoughts. It is daring with sweetness and grace, at the same time this childlike love is also like a soldier in a battle fighting for its love. Endurance of pain for the love comes with an unselfish love between two people. When love remains unchanged between us it becomes the ***petals of us*** though it's no longer with us, the memories, the life spent with each other remains as a fragrance in a flower.

"I pledge my heart in you,

You imprinted yourself in me,

We devoted our love for each other."

Petals of us

"In the morning sun,

in the evening wind,

I can still feel our presence within ".

- Petals of us

"I'm not going to be your glow,

you are not going to be with me anymore,

horrified by this distant image of us,

that keeps moving further away day by day,

this disappearing image of us is reluctant to fail from the game of fate".

- Petals of us

"I still hear your voice behind me all the time,
the softness in your voice,
the warmness in your breath,
made me petrified,
you bowed to my love,
and your voice,
echoed to me "your wish is my command".

- Petals of us

"The tenderness of our love,

that I can never stop admiring it enough ".

- Petals of us

"I caught your starring eyes,

that disturbed my heart for a while,

your stare every minute revoked the rage that I was having

on you,

however, my rage turned into a tale. "

- Petals of us

"Your heart didn't signify me,

mine didn't warn me,

that it will become a part of yours"

-Petals of us

"Tender is your smile,

I wonder if it can become mine,

tonight let it glow,

together we will show,

what our fate should know ".

- Petals of us

"Surrounded by your fort of love,

how do you expect me to escape?

"Bounded by your love ".

- Petals of us

"All my worries were cast away,

when I saw a smile upon your face ".

- Petals of us

"I promise the moonlight tonight,

in this memory of black and white,

that we keep reliving in the amid of our life,

"We trapped ourselves ".

Did you have a clue?

that we will become a prisoner of the love that we have for each other?

- Petals of us

"Even though we are contradictory in everything,

we are awestruck and dazzled in each other's mystery "

- Petals of us

"Silence can never destroy us apart,

when we are with each other's side at heart "

- Petals of us

"In this rainy day, I love to see your glittering face,

that can never fade away,

in my memories, you will stay ."

- Petals of us

"Tender was your heart I always knew,

but I never knew it will be a defender of mine "

- Petals of us

"I didn't expect you to understand me,

but I thought you felt me when we drowned into each other's eyes "

- Petals of us

"The world became blurred around us,

when our eyes met each other"

- Petals of us

"The feel of your love,

thrills me,

surprises me,

how do you do it?

holding me so close to you, even when I am nowhere next to you? "

- Petals of us

"My eyes flickered frantically,

when your voice treated my ears with delight,

now I'm with a smile that could last for centuries and beyond

time.

- Petals of us

Chapter III

Thorn

Thorn is the one that protects the heart of a plant since it's afraid to lose the most beautiful flower we want to cherish is the smile of our beloved though we cannot be with them. We are like a chevalier who guards our loved ones and treasure their memories even though we are no longer in their life.

"Tears dried away,

Heartbeat is about to fail,

Without you in my life is an agony I can never escape ".

Thorn

"Heavenly was your smile,

glittering for a while,

you caught my eyes, and blinded me with your image inside ".

-Thorn

"Tears filled my eyes,

knowing the answer,

I smiled and asked,

are you afraid of me?

or are you afraid of our love

that you hide to the world ? ".

-Thorn

"Tears of sorrows,

years of pain,

you locked my heart with your name".

-Thorn

"I will turn the page for you,

since this is going to be the last chapter of us ."

-Thorn

"The time that is left for us before we become apart,

for the rest of our life,

is like the time that,

I have left to live my life."

-Thorn

"I'm withered,

homeless and hopeless,

as I am banished from your heart,

to the castle of the dark "

-Thorn

"I can't breathe,

I can't dislike when I have to,

life teaches me so much,

even though I became a trampled bud,

sabotaged before its birth,

I will bloom with renewed hope.

-Thorn

"You seem to be too far away,

too far where I don't reflect in your eyes anymore".

-Thorn

"A tiny drop of tear,

surrounds my eyes,

feelings are often untold,

when fear has a hold ".

-Thorn

"Terrors of nightmares

shattered my sleep,

I cried like a child, longing for peace "

-Thorn

"My unfinished business,

why do you keep recurring in my mind without my-

permission".

-Thorn

"Bullets passed through my chest,

when your words shattered my mind into fragments "

-Thorn

"You will always see the sparkle of happiness in my eyes, since our times together keep playing in me like an everlasting marathon ".

-Thorn

"Then and there when I stop and stare,

I get the rhetorical image of us,

that is no longer there ".

-Thorn

"It was just a phone call,

it broke me whole apart,

and cornered me toward the end of your heart "

-Thorn

"Every day, every hour I think about you,

till it scars.

In my heart, I embraced you a million times.

You are drawing closer, I'm drawing farther,

is this our fate's desire?

-Thorn

"Sometimes misery comes with a smile of destiny"

-Thorn

"Read my heart,

not my mind,

it will show you the memories you left behind "

-Thorn

Chapter IV

Flower

The completeness of oneself towards the journey of love, without love it's like their world is without any truth. Love bears all the purity in one's soul and the soul is their flower. The petals of the flower signify the renewal of hope. The flower withholds its immortality through its love. There is no end to love as it keeps blooming in our life. In petals of you, there is the irrevocable, unselfish, sacrificial love.

"The presence of you; is like a fragrance of heaven everywhere"

Petals of us, drags us to the innocence of love, when did it begin? When did it end? It is all unknown in the presence of our innocent love where we dwell ourselves in each other's smile, laughter, sadness, failures, and hope. The innocence of love never tries to hurt since it is as fragile as a "Flower" it withers at some point in everyone's life but the immortality of its presence always lives within us. In this chapter *Flower*, it ends with a note that love is born again in various ways as different paths you take in your journey, it describes love as patient it gives you peace, inspires you, liberates you, to become yourself more and that kind of love is always there it waits for you until you are ready to feel it, always honor it with gratitude.

"Love is stronger than air, that can give you life more than you can ask for,

never be afraid to feel love again when it is presented to you differently"

Flower

"My bundled up emotions are,

exploding without my permission".

-flower

"Memories are stronger than you think,

it has the power to break you,

as well to make you,

and I choose to see; 'It has the power to inspire you ".

-flower

"A small act of love can heal,

an enormous wound".

-flower

"I don't want to erase the memories of our love,

I will let you go,

because I love you more".

-flower

"When there is resolution in love,

the price for salvation emerges itself,

for the cost of the love,

this becomes the birth of first love "

-flower

"In this graceful phase of time,

I can still hear our voices,

our innocent wishes, our silly laughter,

will last like endearing tears of smiles ".

-flower

"I don't want to erase the memories of our love,

but I can let you go,

because it is time to end us,

with a note of goodbye,

this sorrowful moment will heal within time ."

-flower

"Every time we were happy together,

did you know that we loved each other in that entire moment

without any clue,

that someday that moment will stop happening altogether?"

-flower

"We heard the wind blow,

our laughter became louder than ever before,

this is a beautiful symphonic memory,

that will be remembered for centuries and more."

-flower

"Our flower didn't wither,

until our heart stopped to hither,

we gave up on each other forever,

with the memory of our innocent love,

embedded within ourselves as the fragrance of our memories".

-flower

"Our melody of memories,

meddled in my nightmares,

and turned it into a sweet dream ".

-flower

"Though you are not my life story,

you are my memorable story,

to be framed in my life to read ".

-flower

"With colors of our memories that are out on display,

I have miles to go from here,

tomorrow will always be my never-ending hope."

-flower

"The thorns can tear me down,

The creepers could tie me up,

but I will bloom again in this forest of thorns, as a flower to be born ".

-flower

"Be rebellious.

Be charismatic.

Be the ever igniting light to the eyes of the world. "

-flower

"Love is stronger than air, that can give you life more than you can ask for,

never be afraid to feel love again when it is presented to you differently "

-flower

"I became the flower of hope,

when I became aware of the presence of love

around me.

Differently, more faithfully,

I can feel this blossoming love with peace.

The realization that love liberates,

it doesn't contain you,

it releases you,

to the realm of hope and the beginning of a new dawn.

I never felt so strongly before,

I am overflowed with tears of gratitude,

I'm home!".

-flower